IN BLACK BEAR COUNTRY

To Susan and Ted,

dear, generous friends

Maureen

IN BLACK BEAR COUNTRY

Maureen Waters

 An imprint of New Academia Publishing
Washington, DC

Library of Congress Control Number: 2013930475
ISBN 978-0-9886376-0-3 paperback (alk. paper)

 An imprint of New Academia Publishing
P.O. Box 27420, Washington, DC 20038-7420

 info@newacademia.com
www.newacademia.com

To David, a courageous and loving man

Contents

Preface   xi

Acknowledgements   xii

I. IN BLACK BEAR COUNTRY   1

In Black Bear Country   3

Rhythm   4

Premonition   5

Something Else   6

Constructions   7

Hudson Valley Road   8

Nepenthe   9

Singing Tree   10

Snow   11

II. AN ACCUSTOMED PLACE   13

An Accustomed Place   15

On the High Bridge   17

Angels in the Bronx   18

Once Was Christmas   20

A Child's Reach   21

Children Dreaming   22

Metaphysical in Connecticut   23

Rising Water   24

The Wicker Basket   25

Silk   26

Elegy for Agnes' Cat   27

III. JANUARY MOON   29
January Moon   31
Missing, 1975   32
From the Tundra of Experience   33
"Tornado Hits Long Island..."   34
"The loss of anything crucial"   35
Looking toward the Sea   36
Moody   37
Death and the Singer   38
Requiem   39
Brian, 1959—1993   40
Sandra   41
Driving West   42
Gulls   43

IV. PLANTING TULIPS   45
Planting Tulips   47
Woman Listening   48
Eleanor Marie   49
Briana   50
The Spirit of the Place   51
Cold Spring   52
Alouette   53
Hawk Meditating   54
Hudson Valley Rain   55
Small Things   56

V. FIRE WALL   57
Fire Wall   59
War Zones   61
The Grim Facts   63

Uncertainty   64
Lockup   65
Light at New Grange   67
GATES 2005   68
Under the Blue Umbrella   69
Drowned   70
Suegra   71
New Orleans, 2005   72
Encountering Animals   73
The Intruder   75
Point Reyes   76
The Other Side   77

VI. THE FIFTH CORNER   79
The Fifth Corner   81
Oisin's Return from *Tír na nÓg*   82
Gleann Aoláin   83
The Hungry Grass   84
Fionnuala Astray   85
Inishmurray   87
Grandfather   88
"Ancestral Houses"   89
Kidnapped   90
Home Stretch   91
Speechless   92
Midsummer Night   93

VII. "LOVE IS NOT LOVE…"   95
"Love is not Love…"   97
Thinking of Frost   98
Rose Poem   99

Gladiola   100
Antiphony   101
Some Lovers   102
Winter's Night   103
Summer Storm   104
Hudson Valley Autumn   105
A Christmas Carol   106
A Universe of Facts   107
Spuyten Duyvil   108

Preface

The bears, which appear in the title poem, are intended to suggest unpredictability, the mysterious and dangerous aspects of experience as well as the possibility of love. The poems are rooted in a changing landscape ranging from the Hudson River Valley to Manhattan, and further back in time, to the West coast of Ireland, from which the writer's parents emigrated. Arriving in New York in the twenties, they brought memories of famine and civil war as well as strong cultural values. The writer is haunted by their sense of another world, particularly after the death of her son. The poems attempt to work out a reconciliation between radically different perspectives, knowing there is no satisfactory way of doing so. Yet, Seamus Heaney has observed, "As long as the coordinates of the imagined thing correspond to those of the world that we live in and endure, poetry is fulfilling its counterweighting function. It becomes another truth to which we have recourse, before which we can know ourselves in a more fully empowered way."

Acknowledgements

I wish to thank those who read my poems and offered suggestions, particularly Diana Ben-Merre, Agnes Waters, Marie Ponsot, Rosemary Deen, Lee Oser, and David Kleinbard.

I also wish to express appreciation to the editors and publishers of the following where some of my poems first appeared: *Vanguard Voices of the Hudson Valley* ("Constructions"), *WaterWrites: A Hudson River Anthology* ("Driving West"), and *Crab Orchard Review* ("An Accustomed Place").

I. IN BLACK BEAR COUNTRY

In Black Bear Country

Tracks are rare in the high meadow.
They prefer pond shrubbery rich with
blueberries. In spring they may toddle up to
the front door, curious, uncertain what to do.
Driven from maternal dens, they are
unaccustomed to loneliness. And their uncertainty
is troubling in a world where each insect
has its flower, or seems to. They are
the clowns, heads cocked, standing at
the edge of things, waiting for a cue.
For all their size, they move silently,
uprooting boundaries, nudging possibilities.
Theirs is the face at my kitchen window,
hoping for a hot potato. Or an unlikely raccoon
treed by a small dog.

But silence wields a different spell as
day slips through the hemlocks.
As light thins and the barred owl
seeks its prey. A log rolls over, revealing
something other than a clown.
The equation shifts.
What then emerges from the mind or
tenses between the shadows?

Rhythm

Today I found the rhythm, easy and smooth,
that once propelled me through ocean water.
Feeling the prick of cold springs in the depth
of a mountain lake, I was suddenly buoyant,
supple, slipping through the radiant surface
of memory to a plane of possibility.

Experience has become more fluid,
the present more permeable, inclining
to digress or cunningly reverse direction.
The salmon colored dogwood tree
in autumn is rooted in a childhood garden.
This Hudson Valley trail dissolves at a turn
not easily defined. It shifts with the seasons,
circling back along a country road,
along a creek that broadened and plummeted
to amethyst in the distance, an arc of desire
long contemplated but out of reach.

Water has left its imprint on music
evocative, transformative, shifting
the curve of time, restoring lost alliances.
Someone, long absent, is improvising
rhythm and blues, teasing the worn
piano keys, insinuating,
scattering pent-up silence. Take
the risk. Plunge through the music,
find a voice to answer him.

Premonition

Breakfast in October by a frosted window:
maple and shagbark hickory fire
the Shawangunks; barberry gleams
in the long grass. Above the smoking
chimneys hawks tumble and glide.

The season of migrating birds
like shoals of striped or mottled herring,
swallows wheeling past in perfect
symmetry; wild geese dawdling in the fields
rise and settle again, cacophonous,
vaguely human in complaint.

The pitch and taste of light is
gold spilling through the leaves
in this most poignant, most implacable
of seasons.
              Shadows cross
in slow deliberate rhythms
unrecognizable at first in the distance
—one thinks of eagles—
those wings of monstrous birds.
The very air must alter with their coming.
One knows them at once for what they are
at night settling in our trees.

Something Else

A glacier's track; its hollows and eruptions
are plain. Boulders puncture the hillside
where the planking of our house settled
half a century ago. Stone imprints the boundary
of pasture land. Scrub pine and hickory
root in pockets of thin soil. Yet
there are flashes—intermittent, persistent—
of something else.
At the point where hill meets gravel road,
a spring is reaching for the surface,
sifting stone, sowing alien stalks
like dying sunflowers.
Squatting by the roadside, geese breed in
early summer. Muskrat, egret, the small green
heron flourish; trees shrivel down to scaffolding
for beaver huts.
The water level is rising; after snow
a ghostly arc sweeps the corn fields,
touches—still tentative—
the border of our stony enclave.
Something is seeping through.
Something tugs at our mooring.

Constructions
(for Rick)

The house would be cantilevered over the pond
where clear water spilled from a lake beyond
the willows. At twilight there a blue heron
stood sentinel, one foot rooted in sand.

Emptying, the pond spat boulders and entrails
of fish. The crank and whistle of heavy metal
punctured the autumn, tracked through soft earth,
uprooted willows.
                With snow came a desperate
quietness. Until one morning the pond was there
(if not the heron), restored by a visionary
hand on the sluice gate. All winter long
we gloried in transforming water,
saw the moon reflected, the hawk rise.

With spring it vanished at the whim
of a thin man in a black Toyota.

Hudson Valley Road

Death trailed me into the Hudson Valley,
speaking of one beloved to whom I
cannot speak. Her thoughts washed by the river
below her window, she floats above
all sound, silent—it seems—beyond reach.
Can white bellflowers lure her back,
turn her face from the window?
Can she hear music in the tall summer grass,
in the fragrant earth between my fingers?

This road might be hidden in the West
of Ireland, rooks crying out in stony crevices,
or circling the trees. Family ghosts walk
with me through the gray, sweet twilight.
Pioneers of eternity, they come
without reproach, without speech.
We climb to the high pasture, the plain of willows.
Tall and bountiful, drifting in the wind,
their leafy presence is the peace of summer rain.

Nepenthe

Past rose and umber cliffs,
along jagged edge and tumbling curve,
mile on mile we raced a dazzling sun
to reach Nepenthe,
floating high over the Pacific
in a cloud of plaintive shore birds.

What were we then,
we two sisters?
Neither innocent nor gripped by expectation,
free to meet one afternoon,
—folly forgotten, children secure—
on a terrace drenched with hyacinth.

Yet, this was earthquake country.
Beneath poppies and yellow broom
the lovely hills were fissured, dry.
Even as we marked the mute,
single minded flight of cormorants,
we sensed the trembling in the earth,
the sullen hiss of rising tide.

But the moment was too radiant for caution.
Such bliss was in our selves,
such proof against the past,
we plundered the lavish tiers of hyacinth,
assuming beauty was obliged to last.

Singing Tree

Her mode was the subjunctive,
the suggestion of something just
out of reach, waiting to be defined.
She posted books and valentines
and once a golden ring, painted
sailing ships around my bed,
but took me to Manhattan in the spring.
Mischievous, beautiful,
heather in her voice, she opened up
the world like an origami bird or flower
extending the magnet of its bloom.

Thorn in my heart, there is no requiting you.
How willingly I took all you offered
before cancer broke the symmetry
of that perfect face. Dying, you ignored
the fungus lunging for your eye;
traced a shadow of willow green
outside your window.

Snow

As children we searched the sky for snow
better yet—a blizzard sweeping through
brittle trees that froze around us.
The sagging backs of tenement houses,
rusty sign posts, barren streets,
would vanish under blazing sheets
of snow.
       While far below the window where
we dreamed the world, the river churned
a swirling, drifting field of ice.

Snow brought forgetfulness.

Always other than it is,
snow this year quickens the landscape,
unshrouds the dead:

My father deep in snow among the hemlocks
opening up a path, refusing to be
thwarted by the antics of the weather;

A lover unexpected,
filling the doorway on Christmas Eve,
in his arms an extravagance of flowers;

My son in bright red mittens
skating on the silver surface
of a pond.

Snow falling softly.

II. AN ACCUSTOMED PLACE

An Accustomed Place
(the Bronx, 1950)

Why should I go back to that kitchen
with its fickle gas stove and worn linoleum,
a thicket of clothes strung outside
blotting the barest glimpse of sky?

In fact, it's all rubble and ashes,
a few bricks—filched for my garden
from the steps of neighboring houses leaning
toward the river, crumbling, indeterminate.

Yet, once upon a time in winter when
the river wind was stinging ice, we gathered
in that kitchen for bowls of stew served up
with Sinn Fein politics and pots of tea.
Mother read brave fortune in the leaves.

That kitchen shone: Waterford glass
iron pots, the floor scrubbed and polished,
windows washed, the table set.
Our days were framed in homely ritual;
idleness was the privilege of the cat.

Setting an example, Father chanted
lines from Tennyson and Yeats
while he mashed potatoes, stacked plates.
Literature and domestic arts
assumed congenial counterparts.

Barricaded nightly behind our books,
we scholars mused upon the peril of time
in Shakespeare, Keats and Marvell.

The inward eye was trained to see
beyond our narrow purview.

The heart's need was amply met
squeezed round our kitchen table.
Though voices were shouting in the street,
we knew the ease of certainty
in an accustomed place.

On the High Bridge

Red light: Green light. Up and down
seventeen steps to the High Bridge.
On the river below racing sculls
pulled against the tide, yellow boxcars
rattled through the arch beneath our feet,
and death strolled matter-of-factly by.
A thin man in shirt sleeves neatly
dressed in brown stopped, stepped over
the railing and dropped without a sound.

No one moved.
                No one said the word.
The sun shone down
                on everything-as-usual

until the sirens started. Mothers hurried
to the steps, circled all around us.
But no one knew how death had found us.

Angels in the Bronx
(for Agnes)

Of course there were angels.
A phalanx of wings drumming at the
window assured us each a guardian
of our own. Steadfast and vigilant,
they listened discreetly by the telephone,
trailed us through street and corridor,
darting among potatoes and cabbages
oranges and sausages when we
were shopping at the grocery store.

We pictured them in long white robes,
younger than harp-carrying, trumpet-sounding
celestial creatures, but altogether knowing
about unsuspected danger to the soul.

Despite such blessings there was
—I admit—some anxiety in all of this.
How does one accommodate an angel?
At bath time would she avert her eyes?
At night did angels hover overhead,
or should we offer half our bed?

Of course angels were everywhere at Christmas
gliding through the snowbright streets,
voices chanting a silvery *Te Deum*,
an antiphony rising through the spheres,
resounding to delight the dullest ear.

Entering time we lost them;
perhaps, sensing disaffection, they flew away.
When I married there was not one flutter

above the altar, not one whisper
to assure me this was wise.

Yet now as days drift one into the other
 there are portents, perhaps, of reappearance,
a certain brightening at the verge of my experience,
when snow falls softly in December,
when Mozart sings in Latin.

Once Was Christmas

Our Christmas box (provided by
the nuns) was a green striped milk container
filling up with pennies. Resisting tootsie rolls
and bubble gum, we pictured glorious heaps
of pennies turning into dolls and bicycles
before our eyes for children who expected
no surprise on Christmas morning.

We were full of secrets, hiding
 bulky packages in sweater drawers
and underneath the summer clothes.
Rummaging, ourselves, in Mother's closet
while she plaited wreaths of holly.

Night after night we floated skyward
borne aloft on radiant dreams.
Bells chimed in darkened streets below
while snow spilled over all
a nascent sweetness. What did we anticipate
No less than the miraculous?

Once was Christmas.

A Child's Reach

In the top drawer jumble out of reach
was the swollen leather purse of family history:
green passports embossed with golden harps,
marriage license, birth certificates, discharge papers
from the Irish Free State Army.

At four or five
we much preferred the valentine box
with gaily painted ribbons
the scent of vanished chocolates and fresh possibility.
On desolate days, housebound with fever,
we demanded the contents.
And mother would spill them out obligingly
across our rumpled beds:
amber beads and loops of pearl
ivory broach and silver bangles,
a locket wrapped in linen.

Unmollified still
we hunted through silver folds
in which lay coiled
a single strand of bluest blue lapis lazuli.
The chiseled stones cooled our fingers,
hinting at marvels beyond our mute imaginings.
It was the loveliest thing we knew.
Unless, of course, we thought of her.

Children Dreaming

In a trim brick house by a school yard,
my children curl up in Christmas dreams.

Snow is falling on hemlocks, the split
rail fence, what is left of the pumpkin vines.
Silence is so deep I have to listen for the snow
encircling us forever, for all I know.

Neighboring lights have vanished beneath
icy drifts that blow across our street.
And tucked in quilts of blue and white
the dreaming children are mine entirely.

On hands and knees I capture toys,
flocks of bright, provoking creatures
that buzz and squeak and tend to scatter;
devious mice before the Nutcracker.

Between midnight and dawn is still
the hour of fairy and unicorn
when shadows reveal luminous eyes,
benevolent spirits roam the skies.

A clock chimes.
       Too soon.
               Too soon.

Expectation stirs upstairs.
Sunrise blooms in the holly tree.

Metaphysical in Connecticut

It was an eccentric vehicle that MG sedan.
With a sideways motor threatening
 to bolt at the least provocation,
it insisted on coddling and appreciation.

Halfway up the hill to our summer house—
if that car was out of sorts,
if the day was getting hotter—
it would stop, shuddering and snorting.
Backing down politely,
I would praise sundry good points:
the gleaming exterior and distinctive style.
(The kids in the back seat would smile.)
But with a good running start
we'd come soaring up full throttle,
swoop into the driveway,
lights flashing and the kids applauding
our comedy in Connecticut.

Now in retrospect, can it be said
this trial improved their understanding
of the uses of diplomacy
and deferring satisfaction?
Did they begin to grapple with
the concept of uncertainty?
Or far more wisely see
advantages in walking?

Rising Water

Walking home on a country road,
I was glad, at eight, to be out of doors
after weeks of steady rain when
a wall of water came hurtling toward me
an outburst from our stormy creek.
The surrounding wood was strangely
altered; the roadway disappeared.
Plunging on against the current
(feeling pleasantly heroic)
I found we were marooned.

Father meanwhile had not been idle
working rapidly with stone and shovel
 he raised a barrier that forced
the rising water through a wider
channel; saving us from ruin.

The flood retreated all too slowly
filching plants and ornamental
shrubbery; leaving us a muddy road.
It was summer's end before we saw
how much more was lost than was restored.
Our creek was now a bed of stone
whitening irreversibly to bone
After every rain we took the measure
of a trickling pool of water,
but having refused its wild abundance
forfeited its sweeter pleasures.

The Wicker Basket

She lived upstairs with a grand piano
on which stood her husband—Mr. Reagan—
framed in glass. A small energetic
bundle of rectitude dressed in black,
who offered tea on Sunday afternoon
in a flourish of china and silver spoons.
I was lured by apple cake,
freshly baked and smothered in cream.
Thereafter, while the ladies sipped
their tea, I was free to steal
into the kitchen, where lace curtains
fluttered and a not-quite-real canary
in his yellow cage prepared to sing.

One Sunday after cream and apple cake,
I found beside my plate a wicker sewing
basket fitted out with thimble, darning
needle, spools of green and yellow thread.
So, while words sang all about me
I learned to sit politely, producing
row on row of plaintive stitches
round the basket long relinquished
by a daughter, never mentioned.

Silk

In a box of second-hand clothes
passed down through the family
from a friend with a friend who
worked on Fifth Avenue,
I found a dress of pale yellow silk.

Like nothing I had seen before,
so soft, so light and delicate with
a subtle fragrance of its own,
I scarcely dared to slip it on.

Metamorphosis was immediate.
A tree-climbing twelve-year-old
had become a lady of the upper class,
beautiful and fine, one might
even say distinguished, equally
at home in the shops of Rome or Paris.

With my hair pinned up, a touch of
color from mother's cosmetics box,
the effect grew more remarkable:
a Daphne emerging from a laurel tree.

Slipping into green sandals, I moved
gravely toward the kitchen and was greeted
with hot soda bread and a quick
smile: "nice fit." That was it.

But not for Daphne. She had been freed;
her vision widened. She saw herself
a woman with a woman's expectations.
The vines that now were hands might yet
work wonders. The suitors she would find
would be far more reasonable and kind.

Elegy for Agnes' Cat

Ling Ling was a samurai cat,
a rare and wondrous species,
well known throughout the land,
a terror to unwary beasts.
No alien paw dared touch a mouse
if she were prowling round the house.

Yet she was a graceful, pretty kitty
(and sometimes very charming);
many a tom cat yearned for her and sang
of love with fervor most alarming.
But she ignored them one and all;
they were no match for one like her.

Ling Ling was a daring acrobat,
turning cartwheels on the roof,
catapulting through the summer air,
catching flocks of foolish birds
before they knew that she was there.

At night she liked to wander,
pretending to be a Weimaraner,
a bold and cunning hunter but generous
with her booty. Many a hapless bird
and beast reposed at Agnes' feet.

Ling Ling was a formidable creature,
an elegant, articulate companion.
She deserves a place among the stars
hunting tigers with Orion.

III. JANUARY MOON

January Moon

That year the winter sky was brilliant;
terrifying stars pierced my skull,
splintered our snow field. The heavy breath
of absence shook the heart of the oak wood.

There was no explanation.
Just a voice
spelling out your death
until the word itself was clear,
if not the meaning.

Papers: legal, official, explicit
filled the mailbox, spilled onto the floor.
I read them all.
All the post-mortem detail:
age, height, color of hair;
contents of the pockets;
contents of the stomach;
black belt, rubber boots.
(*You* always wore leather.)

Added together: the template of a stranger.
What happened to *you?*
Willful and strong, red haired, humorous,
adventuring through back roads of America,
tracking far off, inscrutable dreams.
The road slipping by.
Time slipping by.
Until one time you failed to notice
that treacherous dip in the road,
the steep curve, the stop sign.

The January moon.

Missing, 1975

A postcard from Bourbon St.,
city of outriders, tall tales, jazz men.
A patch of color on the computer screen,
the connection long ago lost.
Another young man with a blue guitar,
shoulders braced against the wind,
riding a lean strip of highway
from Denver to New Orleans.
With desire a fine gold ring
punched through his ear lobe,
he had to keep moving on.
He would not turn back.

And like the city of his fancy,
fed the whirlwind of his time.

From the Tundra of Experience

On the far side
of this tundra of experience
my small children hide.
Grown old
I am adept at finding them.
Theirs are not the still faces of
photographs arranged in unwavering
chronological pattern
        artful collage
                hermetic memory.

Inhabiting a space theoretically
without consequence or expectation,
these children are not predictable.
At this moment, having gathered
all the lampshades our house affords,
Lee is dallying with planets in
their shining orbits about the sun.
On the lawn Brian is beginning to climb
the voluminous branch of a willow tree.
He cannot know
        that it will snap
           in the prodigious grip
           of a tornado.

"Tornado Hits Long Island..."

Something was about to happen. I knew
before I looked the barometer was dropping.
Silence settled on the street.
Braced against the kitchen door,
I waited.
      Took a breath.
           The roof exploded.
Light filtered through splintered beams,
      broken tiles
           while just outside
our willow tree, voluptuous in depth
      and symmetry,
           lay shattered on the grass.
A snarling wind from nowhere ripped it down,
churned a jagged passage through the town,
      then drifted out to sea.

Neighborhood boys saw things differently,
gathering on our fence before men
      with hacksaws
           hauled away the willow.

Taking the initiative, my young son
wrestled scattered branches,
      got a toehold on
the tipsy trunk and with a flourish
climbed up and through the broken crown,
turned round to the expectant crowd,
      bowed and flexed his muscles.
Playful that day in his audacity,
he eased the fact of blunt adversity.

A gift he thought was his to keep.

"The loss of anything crucial"

If I could reach the top step,
it's not unlikely that
I would find you half-asleep
at the door. It has happened
before. Another boundary crossed,
left behind as you left them
all behind, traveling off-track,
forging your fabulous narrative
until it all fell apart 16 years ago.
Was it l6 years?

The surgeon, fine as tempered steel,
offers the ultimate solution.
A spike driven into the brain,
pushing aside tissue, blood vessels,
implanting electrodes to restore
movement, speech, direction.
"The loss of anything crucial is unlikely."

The express bus has iron wheels,
apparently rectangular.
Jolting through the Bronx, little
seems connected or reliable.
The template has cracked.
What once was home is now a midden heap.
The swans have flown —
perhaps to Central Park.
Block after block is gapped and patched.
The aqueduct that fed a parched Manhattan
is barricaded, shut. The Tower, that
drew the eye like a medieval spire, burned.
Restored, an archive of frayed connections.
A spent force on the horizon.

Looking toward the Sea

I had just turned the umbrella around
to set it more firmly in the sand
when you were gone, running toward the sea.
I caught a glimpse of you slipping beneath
the waves—red hair rippling the surface.
Face to face in the bright salt air
you grinned, neither alarmed nor breathless,
confident, age 3, that I would find you.

You were a solitary swimmer, lured
by the bristling splendor of open sea,
striking out swift and strong
toward nameless horizons.
Until the rip tide caught you.
Like another flouter of boundaries,
Icarus, torn between joy and blindness,
your fabulous gift was not enough.

I still see you waiting calmly at the
bottom of ponds, oceans, rivers overflowing
with rain. Plunging in again
and again, I try to carry you to shore,
but you vanish in the wheeling current
 of death's obscurities.
Like yourself, I cannot grasp
the obvious.

Moody

The moon wanders the January skies,
moody, unpredictable,
drifting tonight behind the gable
of the house, a dim fragment,
shedding the imperative of mutability,
the endlessness of wind and tide.

Lovers, unrequited, no longer respond;
dreams, premonitions are
scattered and found. Indifferent.
Weary. Release her now.
Let her sleep on the gentle slope
of the house, be what she will.
Resist the sinister eye of morning.

Death and the Singer

A singer transfigured by joy
soared over sleepy rooftops,
a topsy-turvy fiddler in Chagall.
Arpeggios hurled from her window
shattered gray tenement walls.

Delphiniums bloomed on the pavement;
summer pines were drenched with snow
at the prelude to Schubert's Serenade,
a note from a Handel oratorio.

Her voice was a silver flute,
a wand of gay enchantment; it seemed
impervious to rust or treachery,
a shield against malevolent reality.

With time she sang for understanding
and against encroaching pain.
In the bleakest hour,
gathering all her power,
she sang against Death.
But here was no compliance.
Death seized one too deeply loved,
leaving her in silence.

Requiem

Then it comes, that final movement:
Libera me, Domine, de morte aeturna.
Her body tenses, desperate to spring
upward, to sound the chord,
soaring above that achievable thing
—the solid contralto line—
as once she was accustomed.
Hurling herself into the gulf of silence
lifting the grief of the world
her own grief
drenched in realms of light.

She cannot resign herself
that this above all is lost;
this impulse as deep as hunger,
all consuming as love.
Triads pounding at her skull
Demand a voice, unfettered, exultant.
Speech is not enough.

Brian, 1959-1993

Past the winter solstice now,
We swing slowly on the axis of night.
Dreams crowd the yellow moon in my window,
And Brian waits behind the beveled glass.
He is watchful,
Waiting for his cue perhaps,
Waiting for me to break the window.

When the world was young,
He died
As a new year was beginning.
Heart scalding trickster, he lingers at thresholds.
If the silences were deep enough,
If my listening eye were keen enough,
Would there be an explanation?

Sandra

We feasted on raspberries, fresh and sweet,
 served that morning with black coffee
on Irish linen. Daniel, aged two,
busy with his calculator was excused.
So I think of you, Sandra, walking in gardens
of roses and raspberries, working
transformations, blithe and intricate,
your poems, your children.

You were our quirky master teacher
mystery writer, student of Spinoza.
A woman luminous with curiosity and delight
noting the rarity of the black walnut tree,
the subtlety of certain lines by Frost.
Cruelly mutilated, you became more beautiful,
like the rich sound of a seasoned cello
resonant to the attentive ear.

There are mornings when I still expect you
with your customary flourish,
bulging appointment book,
wry encompassing smile.

Driving West

Driving west toward the Shawangunk cliffs,
she fixes on a shaft of granite banking
the road as it winds under old growth hemlock.
The house is still shuttered against the snow,
November's cord of wood still heaped against
the gable. Grappling with the unfamiliar,
she will not look at fields, flowering now,
nor the sweep of the tender willow.

A muskrat flicks its tail, tips over into
the swollen pond. Red-winged blackbirds
dart singing through the rushes. But
she will not look at what he loved,
steadfast in abstinence.

Gulls

The gulls
in the grey twilight
scream on the neighboring roof.
Carrion birds,
a scruff of feathers,
a scalpel of bone

The hemlocks
stir in the wind
salt laden, heavy with snow.

And the gulls rise
Muted, elliptical
sweeping skyward
beyond the frozen hemlocks
the caliper of the storm.

IV.   PLANTING TULIPS

Planting Tulips

That year the garden began to die
in mid-summer, though at first
we didn't register the loss. Coreopsis,
begonias, blue delphinium radiated
intensities of light, while under ground
small blind rodents fed on the roots.

Our garden was carved from cow pasture
crisscrossed by stone fences. On
every side stone pressed the surface,
pending the release of heavy rain.

A tulip was a miracle when we first
tackled the soil. Mulching, aerating,
planting with an eye on shifting planes of
sun and shadow floating toward us
from the Appalachian Mountains.

Resisting drought and frost, tumbling
wind and water, our lives rooted in
the garden. If it flourished so would we,
not a reasonable mode of thinking.

More the instinct of desperate people
mired on the hungry plains of Connaught,
battling wild cattle and thorn bush
swallowing their fields.

However we might nurture the aesthetic
that instinct is in our blood as well.
Ten years the garden was a ruin.
This year we planted tulips.

Woman Listening

Young mothers cluster
by the fountain in the park,
nursing infants, retrieving toddlers,
skateboards, tangled up kites,
all the while exchanging
medical and marital advice.

Verging on this maternal circle,
folded in the *Sunday Times,*
I am their rueful admirer.
What else is possible? What can be said
by one whose son, now grown, was doubtless
born in circumstances inadvisable?

Pregnancy was then a hushed event
concealed in layers like a tent,
secured by caution and tradition,
embarazo by admission.

Young women are lucid and exact
the gap between us palpable,
    a consequence
       natural enough
          of a spinning universe.

Still, for all of that,
the marvelous remains intact.

 After the bursting tidal pool
consciousness is like a thread
unwinding from a spool until—
the body's irrefutable expression—
a child curled familiarly, a rare
anemone reaching for the world.

Eleanor Marie

Fierce, beautiful child
come to us in the depths of January
when stars were raw and cold with grief.

Plump, pink little melon
stretching lustily in blue striped pajamas.
Instantly your own creation
hungry, alert, alive, asleep,
given to sudden uproar, sudden peeps.
Inching stubbornly toward the perpendicular,
hind legs foremost,
eager to grasp temptation, eager to start
to taste and test,
draw all within the radius of your heart.

Eleanor at five in silken garments
pirouettes with practiced flair,
a butterfly perches on her shoulder,
a ribbon in her auburn hair.
Now mischief can spring from any corner,
confusion can mar her way.
Still she dances
intricate steps with growing poise,
wholly eloquent is the art she knows.

Briana

Little mermaid swimming toward us,
your navigator a silver dolphin
bound for Gloucester's shore. There
your sister waits in silken slippers,
beckoning while the sea winds roar.

We've glimpsed you dreaming
in your amaranthine grotto,
teasing the timid sea horse
as he whirls and glides.
Delicate fingers luminous, curious
in the warmly pulsing tide.

Little mermaid, bearing hazel nuts
—gifts of wisdom and foresight—
from the gardens of another world,
do you hear us singing through
wave on wave cresting blue and white?
One voice sweeter than any shore bird
eager to ease you tenderly
into the harboring light.

March 2003

"I am not a mermaid; I have two little feet."
Briana, 2006

The Spirit of the Place

My neighboring friend believes
There is a dryad in her trees;
At midsummer she rings them round with fire
And will not cut them down
However much they crowd her narrow hill.

This is whimsy, no doubt
Resisting genetic codes, black holes, computer chips,
a willful, backward arabesque.
Yet, if I were to—momentarily—adopt her stance,
I would say that something stirs our woods as well.

I've long suspected the hemlock.

Seared by lightening, wind and blight,
This is no spreading laurel tree,
No perch for graceful dryad.
The red-tailed hawk has roosted here,
The boreal owl, the buzzard.
Full 80 feet above our roof it climbs.
The crown is bare.
Yet in the sudden light of early snow,
The fragrant branches glisten.
.

At such a time, I might surmise
—if such a thing exists—
That this unlikely, stubborn tree
Could be
The tutelary spirit of the place.

Cold Spring

Persistent rain furrows the soil,
sullen birds twitter in the eaves;
astilbe, columbine, the Lenten rose
unfold tentatively.

It's the boxwood we should look to,
muddling its way through another
unlikely season.

Wasn't the wind of autumn harsh enough?
not to mention the avalanche of winter,
the ice that crouched about the house,
reluctant to let us in or out.

Mangy shrub entangling the hemlock,
loopy tendrils stretching out
in quite the wrong direction.

Where is the elegant form we planned for,
the topiary masterpiece?
What is this ungainly green?

Alouette

There was that chicken.
Alouette, a plump bright yellow,
protruding orange beak
orange feet
blue friendly eyes.
A 5 foot masterpiece
from 3rd grade French,
hatched by a son, now impatient
at the wheel of the car.

Balancing on gapped floorboards,
I was trying to get a grip
on what was left
before the big move
before leaving this house with
its echoes and boxes,
discarded dreams, old clothes.
Not the least was my wedding dress,
 folds of fading organdy and lace,
marked "Good Will" with a little regret.

It was Alouette I most regretted,
but how could I start a new life
with a new man
and an old chicken?

Hawk Meditating
(with due respect to Ted Hughes)

The red tailed, white breasted hawk
studies ruts and furrows
from a vertiginous spur on the shagbark hickory.
Nothing stirs the chill fastness of our woods
where I had stood
contemplating gaps between hemlock trees
in the fearful stretch of winter's afternoon.
Then it materialized, voiceless, soundless,
meditatively perching there.
Perhaps relinquishing the perfect kill.
Proof against the shadow of diminishment,
taking the world as it glides.

Hudson Valley Rain

This spring the rains came hard,
raking snow humped cliffs, flooding
fields with fish from the Wallkill River.
Herring gulls plucked them from the
stubble of last year's corn.
Mesmerized by rising water,
we stood—not quite marooned—
between converging channels; all
around, boundaries were gone.
A flotilla of trees capsized, blocked
the bridge to higher ground.
Somewhere houses were tumbling with the
current. What once was apple orchard
was now uncharted, inland sea.
Huguenots might well appear,
or lost tribes of the Esopus.

Small Things

A maple golden in late October
light. At the root a trickle of water.
We pause as usual. As usual there it is—
a sudden plop of something now hidden,
balancing on a tripwire between seasons
at the precise point a rivulet wells up into
a pool. A space so small a bubble spinning
on the surface contains a point of view.

Peering in the shallow depths among
reeds, chicory, stalks of grass, we cannot detect
the slightest movement. But something is
surely there. Facing up to winter.

V. FIRE WALL

Fire Wall

I fell asleep by the fire wall,
the day's ultimatum—what should be saved?
what could be saved?—rancid in my throat.

Two firemen filled the kitchen,
hoses trained on the window.
Across the alley flame wavered,
having sucked up yards of fabric
from the shop next door.
Was the oil tank in the basement
waiting to explode?

Eyes calculate flames;
wind chokes in the timber. A nod.
They trudge down the hallway,
down four flights of stairs.
It's not over yet.

Thumb prints of smoke in every room.
Wet papers, photographs scattered and soiled,
but the fire wall is holding.

Broadway stands still, blasting alarm.
The Hudson is spurting at intersections.
Pushing against barricades the curious
smile for the press like extras in a
Woody Allen movie.

Midnight. The big trucks begin to move,
lights still flashing.
I fall asleep in my shoes.

Long before dawn scratching, clanking.
Cracks inch across the ceiling.
My bedroom wall is the fire wall.

Fire burns two nights and days.
Teeth are clawing at the plaster.

War Zones

This morning the elevator filled up fast:
tricycles, roller skates, scooters, soccer balls,
children and mothers—an impregnable mass.
I took to the stairs. And watched as they marched
past the front door and onto Broadway.

My tiny granddaughter has the red hair
of my lost son, but her eyes are blue,
her desires infinite.
She dances cautiously, then with abandon
circling the room, singing.
Until the big mirror shows an astonished face,
pink ruffles, bare feet. She settles down
silently to reflect on this.

My sister and I rode the rumble seat
of a second-hand car. Free to scan
the unfamiliar. Free to pinch each other.
Free to climb out.
We climbed trees and fire escapes,
roamed Bronx Park and Pelham Bay,
took the subway to Flatbush to see
what was there.

Children are somber now
buffered in carriages, helmeted on roller skates,
strapped in, wrapped in,
holding safety bars, prepared for anaphylactic shock.

Bombs burst from the front page of the *Times*
They can't read, but they know
it may all end badly.

Have they begun to dream the dreams
of Baghdad and Palestine?
Are they followed by blind naked men,
leashed by the neck; young women smiling,
thumbs up for the camera?

The Grim Facts

I knew it would come—
perhaps like a cunning beast
rending me with yellow teeth,
swallowing flesh and bone with belching
appetite before I could cry out,
attempt resistance, protest
my unaccountable disappearance.

But to be set upon by peevish birds,
vultures masquerading as sparrows,
attacking me sporadically
with swift efficient savagery,
skewering body and mind, leaving me
hallucinatory, half-blind.
An inscrutable Molloy, I totter along
smiling to disguise the damage,
resisting rage that will consume me
finally.

Uncertainty
(the usual report from neurology)

A common metaphor for being,
a gap in the narrative of understanding,
an expectant fool facing the void.

Uncertainty devours her at the core
ensures the steady ebb of patience
and control. Each faltering step
bears the threat of a calamitous fall.

She cannot tie a silken scarf,
or bind her hair with subtle jewels.
A strange affliction mars her speech,
sets her trembling like an aspen leaf.

Elegance is tucked away in bureau drawers,
fragments of much that she has loved
the bright contours of the world,
its aching pleasures, sweeter interludes.

Yet when the chilly winter moon
floods the melancholy trees with light,
dispelling haggard wolves of night,
such radiance confounds her still.

Lockup

On the gurney, one leg twisted under me.
Can't stop choking.
Oxygen pumping. Red light. Red light.
Black man screaming. Fuck you. Fuck you.

Rumpled, incoherent,
hair wrapped in a silk turban,
I look quite mad.
She looks quite mad
  hysterical
        delusional
Nothing wrong with her throat
        medically speaking.
Valium siphoned in drop by drop
        Muscles relax.

What next? Psychiatric evaluation
a.k.a. *The Lockup*!
Only they don't tell you that.
Truth decompresses slowly.

A surround of bilious green
plastic chairs, windowless walls.
Mad people in green paper caps.
I hold on to my turban.
A nurse behind bars
three guards
watching the clock
watching us
smothering in green fog.

Don't speak. Don't move.
Keep breathing.
Avoid their eyes.

The clock ticks behind bars.
Whatever time it is, time is up.
They're locking up.
They're locking us up for the night.

A resident, professional, poised,
in well tailored clothes, takes my measure:
a rag tag bundle in a silk turban.
(Should I mention my three degrees?)

How to explain,
despite appearances,
despite a little trouble breathing,
that's me under there.

Terror can be restorative.
Turn the key…
Words unlock.

Light at New Grange

This morning a sea change,
 a reckoning.
At 4 a.m. the mood is spectral, strange.
In my designated chair
I wait. Immobilized.
The sullen panes of glass turn back
An unaccustomed face
Too white, too thin.
The beloved and familiar have scattered
or conceal themselves.
A fine old book's a burden in my hands.

Is this then the farthest point?
Does the piercing eye of winter light
flood the corbelled passage of the Boyne?
Or can I still return,
My own Eurydice,
To warmer climes?

GATES 2005

In the bleakest of Februarys
23 miles of "saffron,"
(or is it "orange"?)
23 miles of swirling color
23 miles of gates.

Whatever it is, it is
ticking with superlatives.
The engineering is precise.
And the scale is large.

Why quarrel with such
enterprise? This thumb
in the eye of the beholder?
This apotheosis of Central Park?

The public is amused. Here is
matter for speculation,
a pied piper of playfulness.
And the scale is large.

Why not enjoy the irony of
gates in a locked up city,
doors and windows bolted tight,
avenues blocked, traffic stopped?

The Gates of Christo and Jeanne-Claude
are paradoxical: open
and closed. Art and counterpart
tweak the metropolitan nose.

Under the Blue Umbrella

The train lurched forward.
Clinging to a pole I crashed to the floor,
wet feet all around me.
I lay there watching those feet
until I was hauled to a vacated seat
while a chorus inquired relentlessly:
"Are you okay?" What could I say?
My head had cracked in two.

I smiled, attempting disguise, but
the lady in green knew better.
"You can't be too careful my dear."
I kept smiling while the fellow beside her
began to expose his unruly anatomy.

At an opportune stop, I got off in the Village.
Friends were meeting—I didn't know where.
I walked east. I walked west. But didn't despair.
Something was sure to turn up. And they did,
stepping out no doubt from a Tennessee Williams play,
a gentleman and his lady with a blue
beach umbrella, perfect for a rainy day.
And was that me, Blanche DuBois,
accepting the kindness of strangers?

Arm and arm we sauntered along, conversing
on metrical form in *The Iliad* when there in
the fog beamed *Le Pot au Feu*, which I soon
recollected was the place designated
for rendezvous. My escorts were surprised
that we wouldn't be dining *à trois*. Expressing regret,
"so glad we met," I bade them farewell
under the blue umbrella.

Drowned

The fortunate technology of distance
allows this phone call,
its cadence of measured civility
inching across an abyss of conjecture,
whole narratives drowned and abandoned
in bewildering memory.

Miles to the north villages stand
deep in water. When the surface clears
in late October, one sees houses, a barn;
streets wind toward a center.
The notion of a place, a home persists,
persisted even as cascading water
swallowed them whole, flowing in and
downward, tunneling beneath the Hudson
to quench the desperation of a city.

The inconstant tide of our affections
is churned by broken glass,
cracked tiles, kegged dynamite,
whole chunks of the impenetrable
resisting containment or release.
But we know what's down there
the missing figure, the double x.
On the mildest summer day we can't grasp
that equation so charged with meaning.
Nor do we want to.

Suegra

Here are fresh oranges, plum cake,
a basket of firewood. She slowly unbends,
glances in my direction, nods acceptance.
The beautiful children dangle from the sofa,
flashing cards, smiles, inviting me
to join their unfathomable game.

My place here is unfathomable.
I cannot decipher the cues, resolve
such reticence. The children know.
It is the steel at their core, the sharp
gaze in their hazel eyes.
Each step across their carpet is completely
new. At what point do I turn?
What is it that swells and smothers?
What was my fatal error?

Night falls. The children scamper upstairs
The firewood stands in a corner.

New Orleans, 2005

Day after day the city drowns.
The dimly human cling to rooftops, trees;
the reluctant dead are floating rubbish.
Young men hurl themselves from helicopters
snatching up, one by one, tenants
of this unexpected nightmare.
Hooded men snatch jewelry, money, guns.
Houses torched, murder and rape
seep through the floorboards. The aged
drown in attics, barricading their doors.

Less than systematic in the absence of landmarks,
search and rescue teams trail the escaped
or drowned. In football stadiums thousands wait,
sleepless, blistered, smothered in heat, sewage;
no water, no food. They start walking to
nowhere.

Encountering Animals

On the Snake River we heard
the melodious cry of a young eagle,
bewildered by the impulse to fly
beyond familiar nesting trees.
A drowsy moose ignored us
though we startled the swans and
elk foraging among the willows.

A horde of bison startled us, stalled
and gridlocked in our rental car.
Seasoned performers, stamping and snorting
they stalked back and forth between
fenders, halting obligingly while
we captured them with throwaway cameras

II

Northeast from the sweltering valley floor
rose the peaks of the Grand Tetons
restless, shifting skyward, shrouded in snow.
The glittering lure of high country
stirred the wilderness in us.

Ascending through shafts of clear blue light,
we passed meadows where lupine bloomed and
glacial rock tumbled into lodgepole pine,
dragons might have inhabited so rare a world,
guardians of meditative solitude.

But with light failing, we blundered
onto dangerous terrain. Frost
burned our eyes, set us spinning
on the rim of some gigantic wheel.
Which was earth and which was sky?

Ice laden hills rolled across the horizon,
Nothing human offered a direction.
Fog settled in among the trees
while far below the valley disappeared.

Desire had compelled us farther than
we were prepared to go. Edging down,
we hunted more congenial ground,
when from a ridge above our heads
a mountain lion, more shadow than a cat,
glided across our path, and dropped
over the frozen cliff.

The Intruder

This morning outside our kitchen window
a small owl perched on the woodstove chimney.
More eye than rusty feather
as still as stone.
It fixed us with a baleful gaze,
whatever was the meaning,
some curse or worse?
Blue jays all around were screaming.
Too late.
The creature was out of place,
trailing legendary demons, lost souls, evil omens.
So small and so keen a predator.
What murders had been perpetrated
while we were dreaming?

When at last we turned to household tasks
the owl retired to a hemlock,
sank its talons in and meditated.
What claims were violated?
As wings circling overhead
beat with steady menace,
flocks of sparrows darted near
then rapidly aware in fear.
The intruder never stirred,
By noon it vanished
undeterred.

Point Reyes

We were nearing the lighthouse
poised on the lip of Point Reyes,
the sky a whorl of sea birds
driven east by oncoming storms.

On the beach a ring of watchers
gazed toward the wind whipped horizon
where mermen on blue and vermillion sails
flew over the crest of the sea.

One was precise, an arrow aimed at
the lighthouse; the other soared on a timpani
of wind, a dancer turning arabesques,
his audience mesmerized on sand.

Above the high water mark,
carved in granite, a marine chart
noted the danger of rip tides
and the occasional great white shark.

The Other Side

We knew it was there
spotted by geese swerving
sharply from the north.
Within the dense rebuff of trees
water plunged through hoops of light
scattering spittlebugs and fish.
What was the source?

Night sounds floated across
a barred owl, a coyote;
nameless sounds stirred the underbrush.

Was this division merely mind
floundering across primitive terrain,
 insisting on signs and portents?

Winter might have provided
definition, leaves crumbled,
trees stooped in heavy snow.

But nothing seemed as it truly was,
or as we had expected,
this stiffening field of ice
obscuring our horizon.

VI. THE FIFTH CORNER

The Fifth Corner

One on each side.
Simple enough
 this accustomed stance,
but we can't seem to situate
parallel markers in comfortable folds.
The surface is somehow larger
as if it stretched
in unforeseen directions
last night.
Here are more bulges
than molehills in the lawn.
A fifth corner has emerged.

A fifth province the Celts insisted
lay midway between earth and heaven.

Oisin's Return from *Tír na nÓg*
(from the Irish, "Land of Youth")

The bridle snapped. He plunged
through the gap she warned him of
in his long dream of happiness.
Bones shrank; joints twisted and cracked
muscles and sinews stiffened and rasped.
He dropped to his knees.
Seeing nothing, he saw it all.

The authorities retrieved what was left
of the hero; labeled him senile, hopeless,
providing small tasks to fill his day.
He turned disputatious and intractable,
mocked their grim certainties,
remembering he had been young.

Gleann Aoláin

The road was a narrow shaft
tunneling through fields where
cattle shifted in a fog of stinging insects.
Grasping at fence posts I stumbled
toward the house;
underfoot, bog water, thistles, dung.
And no boots.
Walls of gray Connemara stone
wisps of thatch where the roof had been.
At the storied source
an anonymous interior
a stunning silence.

Sun flooded the slope where barley grew,
where men were hunted down
and children starved
In *Gleann Aoláin*
even the ghosts had vanished.

But the living carried with them
a cage of words
whistling blackbirds
set free by the Atlantic.

The Hungry Grass

A bitter malady is in our blood;
the subterranean fury of abandoned
seams of coal with time and pressure
must explode. In every generation some
are stricken, sealed in pain, burrow into
 isolation like the famine Irish
shutting their hearts against the world.

Children, starving, mouths filled with
deadly grass, buried in a field at night.
No hope of justice. No recourse.
Their very names were lost. Too
terrible a thing to speak aloud.
But carried deep in memory:
a severed head preserved in peat.

Carried into exile with music
and stories, cherished custom and belief.
Unforgotten. Unforgiven.
No respite, but silence and retreat.

Fionnuala Astray
(After *The Children of Lir*)

At first they understood,
despite the feathered form
and clamorous wings,
the curving ivory neck.
She spoke the language of kinship,
scattering a web of silver notes
that drew them to the lake shore
where she drifted, transfigured,
Lir's only daughter.

Setting aside sword and shield,
they listened unprotesting, enchanted;
forgot their grief that
she was lost to them forever.
A creature now of water, wind and sky,
exiled from earth,
her shining face;
a shadow from the past.

She foresaw no hand extended,
no hero to lift her from captivity.
The curse that bound her fast
must in the end release her.
But to what purpose, to what stranger
could she yield her heart?
At night sheltering in the reeds
she felt the pangs of bitterness.

Years passed; seasons erupted
cycle by cycle through the trees.
Generations came and went,

grew accustomed to her strangeness,
the faint echo of her music, her tremulous speech.
When icy blasts swept her out to sea
Someone remembered her name.

So began the legend of Fionnuala,
Lir's only daughter,
borne on the current of time
before time; valiant and beautiful,
shrouded in virtue,
they now proclaimed the will of God.

Inishmurray

Nine miles from the enchanted
slopes of blue Ben Bulben,
fogbound in treacherous seas.

This is no fabled isle
of transformation and desire:
monks in coracles seeking the miraculous,
vengeful Mael Duin stymied in the land
of youth, the fragrant isle of women.

Among broken monuments
tenacious life withdrew from history;
offered ritual acts of work and prayer, and
heaped one altar high with cursing stones,
blue, speckled *clocha-breaca.*

The *Annals* speak of scholars, then of
Vikings who left their mark in blood
upon an altar stone and vanished.
The islanders eluded the chance
marauder, reclaimed their solitude.

Inside cashel walls, among
beehive cells and standing pillar
stones, they burrowed in and downward,
sang their songs, gave birth to children,
held their outpost in the Atlantic

My own people among them,
kings of Inishmurray. Abandoned now ·
but for the windblown sea birds.

Grandfather

There is no picture of my grandfather.
He generated silence: "no need to speak
ill of the dead," and many children.
A man at odds with his neighbors,
at odds with life, which coffined him
prematurely; turned him back to the
green fields, where there was
no forgiveness,
no resurrection.
A thin man with a ginger mustache
breaking his back, breaking up sod
in those green fields.
How palpable now
his fear,
his fury,
the handkerchief bound round his head.
At the finish he relented,
fell in love with his seventh daughter,
beautiful like the first who,
dying, cracked his heart.
At Christmas
he brought her shoes of softest leather.

"Ancestral Houses"

Lissadell, a ruptured link
to history, poetry and misrule.
Home to autocrats and outcasts
sworn to integrity; haunted
by tales of infamy and murder:
the Gore-Booths of Sligo.

Yeats took tea there in the light of evening,
remembering in the aftermath of vision
the grace and power in those gray walls
the delicacy of the women.

For generations my people served them,
curried their horses, planted, harvested,
carried their goods from market to market—
survived the famine.

Father rode bareback as a boy
through fields of poppies and flowering plum
glimpsed halls festooned with gay embroidery
silver dishes and old mahogany
a grand piano at the center of a room.

In time war rained down blood and irony.
High roof beams burned
the landscape shifted with calamity

Gore-Booth stood by an open window
unbound but pledged as hostage
to a 16-year-old Volunteer.
Shifting his rifle, Father offered tea
on that late autumn afternoon;
measured the cool authority of the man
against his certain ruin.

Kidnapped

She never forgave father for dying.
In fact, she never forgave anything after that.
She stopped speaking to God,
summoning the dead directly when
there was something on her mind.

She raged and raged as life closed in,
relentlessly stripping away her treasures:
the bright red Ford with faulty ignition
the rambling summer house and garden.

One morning she cornered the postman, insisting
she had been kidnapped; pieces of her self
were missing; more were disappearing every day.
When he stood there speechless,
she smashed the bedroom mirror and
shut her window against the singing birds.

I thought of Keats' swallows gathering in
the mellow evening light of autumn
and of my father's enduring stoicism.
Then nurses forced me to remove
the wedding ring from her beautiful hand.

Home Stretch

The brisk, determined stride was him all right.
We were sure even as he stepped out of
Manhattan, out of the subway, onto the footbridge.
From our window perch across the river,
we watched him growing more distinct: head up,
paper in hand, jacket open to the wind.
Sighting us, he waved the banner of the
News. Time to put on the tea. Time
to tell what we feared to tell
                              about the letter
stamped in Mullaghmore, drumming the sound
of death, the wrenching heart of death although
the woman in the photograph was old.
But how could we confront him? How
retrieve the moment he had labored toward?

Speechless

We always send flowers, trusting
the eloquence of violets or a white rose
to speak what the heart has framed but
cannot muster. Tending birth and death and
all the hazards, all the happiness between,
we offer flowers.

Day after day we contend with tribal
volubility as though silence
were defeat or dissolution. Yet
we hesitate, stumble, clench the word
between our teeth as if to give it speech
would rupture our grip on history,
restore the order we were bred into,
rituals salted with too much grief.
Unreasonable, impossible, the magnitude
of those beliefs.

Midsummer Night

The clown stepping back
cannot say what he has seen.
This night's performance was rare
beyond measure, beyond reason.
Chance plucked him,
—was it chance?—
sent him tumbling into the lap of
the uncanny. Debased, translated, but
a player still. Willing to outface mockers,
wrestle with Lion or the Hornéd Moon.
His eye if not his voice redeems him,
reflecting, still, a boundary crossed.

VII.   "LOVE IS NOT LOVE…"

"Love is not love
Which alters when it alteration finds…"
(Shakespeare, Sonnet 116)

Or so I once believed
—as in the numinous or celestial form—
but practice leads me to concede
that the dearest love must falter,
which is not to say that it will end,
for the wheeling years that cycle
between pleasure and despair may yield
an understanding, ardent as well as rare.

And do we not retain,
like crystal fused in meteorite,
traces of all that we have borne
of beauty or virtue bearing consequence?
Is this not apparent to discerning love
however freely spent?

Thinking of Frost

In birch country nature's first green is gold.
But here before the purge of winter,
We are circled in sheaves of gold.
Leafy profusions baffle the horizon;
Shagbark hickory swallows the Shawangunk cliffs.

Desire like a sudden wind
Ripples through the afternoon.
Your voice quickens, pulsates,
The accretions of 30 years exposed between us.
Known and yet unknown, a man aloof
Among his teeming books
Regards me now, remembering…
Do you remember?
The clamorous early sky over Eggemoggin.
And beneath our window
The red spinnaker breasting the tide.

Rose Poem

I can't manage them.
Bright, capricious blossoms
thrusting petals through pine
and rhododendron, trailing
sprockets of leaf and thorn.

This morning I took the pruning
shears, mounted the gable and
grappled with the upper branches,
but the fibrous vine proved
too thick for the blade.
What could I do
but let it alone?
Heavy scented, outrageous,
out of all proportion to the house.

Gladiola

Between us on the table
a green stalk of gladiola stands in a glass
the coral buds extended.

In the street a woman moves
brisk and furred through the cool November night.

Within we are at leisure
to drift through sunny afternoons
oblique and tender
as the slow tide stretching full upon the land.

Your voice in the mellow light
catches the rush of birds,
the bristling August sky of Camden.

You draw me toward you,
a subtle fluctuation,
along the bright trajectory of summer past.

Antiphony

You turn up the lamp and regard me thoroughly.
Shrugging off uneasiness
        along with blue lingerie,
I pivot on one heel, reaching for certainty,
        framed in the instant
 like the brown woman bare breasted on your wall.
The caverns of your face mock solid objects.
        You invite motion,
easing me under the rose coverlet.
Your energy shatters a too coherent center:
        Mine, depends on it.

Some Lovers

Some lovers have the gift
—providing they were passionate men,
however disquieting in the end—
of subtly interceding
when you have drifted into the abyss
of tedium or loneliness.
Indeed they may be summoned forth at will,
erasing the prints of sorrow from a room
or confusion about whom you have become.
They hold the secret of sweeter seasons
when desire wakened you at late night hours
and pressed you to the earth
among the tumbling flowers.

Winter's Night

On a winter's night
—How many years ago?—
we slipped away from time to this inn,
venerable and bright with bristling fires
sprays of holly, creaking floors.
On the wall above our bed,
white with crisp embroidered linen,
a Norman Rockwell print
beamed at us then as now.

Awash in silver froth,
I settled in the depths of
a prodigious porcelain tub,
lion paws extended, while you
the artful instigator, paused discreetly,
noting the eccentric design of the wallpaper.

Tonight, keyed to the hollow singing of
the moon, a door closes silently.
Not only time has snared us,
but the unyielding fiction each is wedded to.

Summer Storm

Summer storms are fierce in these hills
dense with oak and ravaged hemlock.
Lightning has scorched the roof, burned up
telephone cables, left them darkness,
silence. Shutdown complete.

Last night in the midst of thunder,
he came to the bedroom door,
a familiar, practiced lover,
descended from his eerie
and the solitude of meditation.

His gaze curled round her, embracing
thirty years and all those years contain
of passion, sorrow and deference.
What has been has found its depth
deployed like Appalachian fire,
and spiraling forth regales the earth,
loosestrife in a summer meadow.

Nerves and sinews remembering,
her skin grew fragrant, softer, silken
as he, entering the room,
sensed the radiance in her blood,
penetrated the dark between them.

Hudson Valley Autumn

Not the ease of mellow fruitfulness;
but the pungent snap of Macintosh and
Cortland apples, bins heaped with pumpkins,
squash, turnip, kitchens reeking of hot soup.
Blowsy sunflowers droop by the road.
Ravens croak, hawks swoop and turn
above the house awash with light.
October's plum, russet, yellow leaves
are whirled away. The willow
a chandelier of early frost.

Poised on the cusp of winter,
there comes a radiance,
a resistance to the turning earth,
a will to stay awhile.

A Christmas Carol

The lead soprano, beautiful as
 her voice, stands before a scrim of
silver trees, a compelling archive
of memory. One can picture her
a child, reaching, pianissimo,
for those silver notes. A Yule log
simmers; perhaps a plum pudding.

As we circle toward midnight,
Adeste Fideles resonant in the ear,
chimes ring out, candles are ablaze.
And love seems now less tentative,
the sting of grief assuaged.

Still it comes, the ecstatic, precise pitch,
the visionary note at our beginning.

A Universe of Parts

At the finish we lose everything,
but days are now perplexed by
what refuses to be gone. The bridge
that spanned the river of childhood
stands firmly in the forefront of my mind.
I cross back along the cracked
brick pavement to gather what was there:
pieces, a thousand pieces—a puzzle
framing the bridge to what is now.
How surely a form emerged from
disparate shapes and blots of color.
How confident I was that it would all
add up to something recognizable and true.
Solid as the gray stone house we lived in
(long gone to weed and empty space).
Yet certain things remain, insistent
as lampposts on a deserted street.
While their coordinates are now elusive,
there is assurance in this universe of parts.

Spuyten Duyvil

Sunset high over Spuyten Duyvil,
the tide running east from the Hudson
through a dredged-out ship canal.
We two mesmerized before
the conflux of bridges, rivers, trains
rumbling beneath our feet; echoes starting up
from every corner of our lives.

What fixes the eye?
A parabola etched on the horizon.
A Delta flight arcing in from the sea
bound for the coast of Utopia.
The rosy plume fanning out
seems at first an image
of something lost and marvelous,
years released into the air,
 an eagerness of spirit
I thought was only youth
dazzled by the redwood spires
of Muir's Wood,
burning and yet alive.

Resisting age and death,
the splintering impact of this minute,
there is an effulgence east or west
—if one will claim it—
these rivers to which we have returned,
the sea gulls wheeling above the tidal basin,
a full moon startling the sky.

CPSIA information can be obtained at www.ICGtesting.com
Printed in the USA
BVOW011332210213

313816BV00003B/4/P